THE SWORD OF TIME

I-III

HANK FISHER

Beaver's Pond Press, Inc.
Edina, Minnesota

The Book of the Law, quoted on page 20 and referred to on page 45,
was written by Aleister Crowley.

39/500
H.F.

ISBN 1-890676-69-1

Library of Congress Catalog Number: 00-105550

Printed in the United States of America.

04 03 02 01 00 6 5 4 3 2 1

The Sword of Time

Book I: The Sword of Time

Book II: Conquest

Book III: Fulfillment

And if we come to the heart of the mystery,
perhaps we should say that the truly eloquent
man is a sane man with power to communicate
his sanity.

—Emerson, *Society and Solitude*

Book I: The Sword of Time

Book II: Conquest

Book III: Fulfillment

Book III: Fulfillment (Cont.)

Book I:

The Sword of Time

Fiercely Alive, Despite

Self-Counsel

Force a fierce flower
Into your sky,
This mound.

To hold life
(Hated need)
Your heart's limbs
Must be buried, bound
(The body's forced you
To a living grave).
No sun,
No bright sky (for you)
But poetry.

Pierce the stifling earth.
Open, joyfully, pain's flower
—Some ear
Will grasp the petaled wonder
And feel beneath,
The tight and tangled roots.

Only pain's tongue
Can force the flower
(Starkly veined)
That grows
Immortal;
Some living ear
Will hear—and pluck—
For pain tears
At life's root.

The Garden of Eden

Beauty has closed its terrible door;
My barren fruits
Find no admittance.

His face has turned;
His flesh has no use
For mine.

Loyalty

Defy the tyrant behind the sky!

Poet

Heavy stone tops heavy stone
—A temple to my pain;
Hate, too, has spires
That pierce the heartless sky.
High up, my screaming stone
Cuts against the indifferent wind;
My chorister, chipped rudely
On that windy peak,
Soars, a frozen agony,
Soars, on outraged wings.

Fierce Muse

Fierce muse,
Chain me.

I sing better
Straitened on a block,
Sweating for your voice
To cut revealing
Through my being
Till I shriek
Fresh blood
From my mouth.

The Sword of Time

Sorrow

Just as sorrow is the source of evil,
Self-ignorance is the source of sorrow.

Nietzsche

Nietzsche

—No stone of gold,
But angry iron—

I stare in sadness at your broken face,
I see what you've become:
A wandering misery, whose lightning can neither illuminate
Nor console.

Heart's peace means more than biting hail;
To the broken heart, I say,
Farewell.

A Nightmare

A Nightmare, staring,
Looked at me—

I: You have no eyes;
It's I who see.

Those I Love

I become those I am in love with:
Socrates, Pan,
Truth, a neighbor boy,
The poets who have taught me song,
The minds who think in shining phrases,
The hearts, profound,
Who warm my life.

To an Exorcist Weary of the Call to War

Not every fear imprisons
The innocent fire
Or blocks the shining
Of beauty desired;
Some are mere terrors,
Best left to howl
In their emptiness.

Mere Wealth

Mere wealth
—It makes me laugh—
Dull acquirement,
Worthless substance,
Not pulsing flesh
And noble coin,
A king's expanse,
A lover's yes,
The rich and solid ground
Of fire's gold
And heart's respect.

Fear of Poetry

after reading Emily Dickinson

Doomed—to Light—
A poet's—lie—
The Heaven—of words?
Who would not—die?

The Sword of Time

"I am the magician and the exorcist,"
Says Beauty;
The tyrant cannot create,
Nor can the crucified cast out.

Heart's slaughter
Saves no one;
Raise Joy's sword
Or none.

Note:
Line 1 is from *The Book of the Law* II:7.

Lonely as Mud

Lonely as mud, I saddled my broken heart
And rode to the spring from which beauty and contentment flow.
"Contentment is flame," said he.
"Beauty's a sun," said she.
"We are Eden's flaming sword. Become us."

I laughed, and
My heart was whole.
I drank, and
My soul was flame.

No, Nietzsche,
Not man, but the divine in man,
Is the measure of all things.

Prayer

Archer Death

Archer Death,
Protect my silent hearthstone
With your arrows of unbroken flame.

With your most genuine,
Kill self-pity;
With your most joyous,
Kill self-hate;
With your most beautiful,
Kill self-ignorance.

Archer Death,
Protect my sanctuary.

Book II:

Conquest

Mr. Eliot

What use, Mr. Eliot,
Precise language
If that described must crumble into dust?
(And—so you remind us—it must.)

Besides, the essence of one's era
Is not captured in accurate statement
(An oracle is not a reporter;
 The oracle is joyous insight).
The only record, therefore, of consequence
Between the self and its era
Is beauty's,
Swift, delight-filled, shining beauty's;
Painfully lifted dust is only painfully lifted dust.

If the object does not exist (it does not)
How can that sifted upon it (dead in itself)
Exist apart from that it is sifted upon
(Its form is that it is sifted upon)?

How sad to meet Mr. Eliot
(whose mind was bent over dust).

Knowledge

Knowledge does not exist
Because perception is oneness-with
(Joy in one's own oneness
  Relating perfectly to all joy
  From that oneness).

Knowledge does not exist
Because knowledge is description
(Description is not existence;
  What is is existence.
  But what is is undivided:
  Being is oneness-with).
Knowledge does not exist.

Great Are the Ruins

Most grim and grey
We sat, the wander flock,
Most grim and grey.
No! Not even on an hour! [*despairingly*]
      Not even on an hour!
Why cannot the door open?

We listened while the song sang,
The song sang and the slant-feather
Presented its haunting.
Oh, what could we do?
      What could we do?

Great are the ruins
Of that that falls,
Yet small the cry of the broken.
Who can lift the mountain
That has plummeted?
Who can lift the mountain
Crowned no longer
With gold?

That Without

A materialist sees only that without;
A moralist judges only by that without.
Love sees the truth within;
Love judges by the truth within;
Silent consciousness penetrates all barriers.

Dionysos by Apollo Divided

The joy of mortality is immortal consciousness,
The wholeness of memory,
The laugh of history;
Lovers embrace within immortal love.

The agony of birth, the agony of death
Are misconceptions
—Hell is profound in its error.
Birth is beautiful;
Death is beautiful;
Both are forms of continuous joy.

The Tender Skin

The tender skin,
Through which flows the blood of life,
The blood of death

—no ticking scientist, no dead watch,
  cold, observant,
  can steal the fire of my soul

Nor can the body (however broken)
Keep its owner
From the temple of contentment.

Homer's Heroes Are But Frauds

Serenity is the goddess of war;
Contentment is the god of thought.
Scheming is not content;
Rage is not serene.

This Terror That I Face

Is this terror that I face
So terrible,
This terror that is but myself?
To think the torment I have fought
So bitterly
Is but the triumph of my standing self,
Its innocence, its honest ecstasy;
This wrestling match, so long embraced,
This wrestling match, my secret history
—Two opposed, where none can win,
With bitter swords and howling brands,
Two opposed, where both must lose
(Love's fire—dark Hephaestus—claims
The iron crown of each
To forge his cup of lasting gold)

Who, then, can I claim to be
When this self-stifling tournament
No longer claims my destiny?
Who, then, can I claim to be
When wholeness is my sanctity?

Great Death

Great Death, we have forgotten yours
Is a house of laughter—not apples of dust,
With bitter seeds, and harsh and tasteless rinds,
But golden apples, spheres of centered joy,
Transform.
The mortal cannot remain;
Its bliss is to live the moment
Along the path that is eternal,
To eat and to be eaten
With contentment's mouth.
Timid mortal, die to joy,
And she will hold you, ever,
In her arms.

On a Public Bus

Here, in the immediate world,
Where the joy of the celestial Mother
Is between each of us,
Where the temple is the present heart,
Not tomorrow's, not yesterday's,
Where beauty shines instantly,
Child of the moment,
Out of the centered self,
Here, in the immediate world,
Beauty to beauty,
Joy to joy,
Athena extends her shining city,
Her contented, her self-triumphant home.

What of It?

So the intellect comprehends
—What of it?
What of the mating of vitality with vitality
And what of their shining oneness,
The transforming world?
Not only are the eye and the object a unity
(O Wordsworth!)
But description
(Whether accurate or inaccurate)
Is nothing
Compared to the joy of mating flame;
The genuine fire—its laughter, its contentment—means more
Than the lonely bones of painfully measuring, heart-stifling
Comprehension.

Oneness

To kiss the face of gold,
To fill its mounted depths
With seed,
Is that oneness?
To be the face that beauty kisses,
To be the depths that beauty
Mounts,
Is that oneness?
To be the beauty kissed,
The beauty mounted,
Or beauty kissing,
Beauty mounting,
Is that oneness?
Oneness
Is the circle's mystery,
The joy, the stillness,
Pursued, pursuing;
Oneness is the gold
Of shining time.

The Struggle to Make a Monument of the Tortured Past

Bleeding, discontented body,
Demented worm
(Unable to stretch ahead,
 Unable to stretch behind,
 Unable to crawl within your meagre now),
What golden fishhook
Will feed you to that stronger death,
That swiftly darting, blissful-swimming
Fish of constant joy?

Has petty time fooled you
With its raging ghosts, its spectres
Unaware of time's beginning?
Self-embrace
(Before, upon, and after
 These little wars, these crowns and penances,
 Of this, the false and empty present)
Self-embrace, its centered bliss,
Is time's beginning.

Centered bliss
Means more than fame
And more than the pen's cathedral
Built with pain
And bitter emptiness;
Yet joy in one's ability
And joy in being loved for excellence
Both triumph and sustain.
The artist is the god within
(He does his daily tasks like any mortal);
His triumph in his chosen medium
Is noble
Where his beauty shines,
His bliss proclaims.

The Poet's Task

To be
The deliberate tongue
Cutting the cold stone
Of remembered experience
—Is that the poet's task?
Or is it to be the song spontaneous,
Where memory mates with melody?
Poets, poets,
Precise, yet free;
Truth's champions,
Truth's children.

Conquest

Even God is not enough
If one is not that one small spark of Him
That is oneself

—Yet how to embrace that which is one's own
   If one condemns all conquest,
   If one condemns all self-broadening expansion?

Need is not enough, righteousness is not enough
To wear the crown of conqueror;
Self-shining, self-joy
—They are enough;
They are the Yes of every honest king.
Every self
Radiating self-joyously its inner light
Is conqueror,
Is self-extender of its domain;
Those joyous feed the best
In themselves and in those around them
(All joy, like all divinity, is one);
The swords of beauty vary
(One man's palace is not another's);
Yet Beauty, for all, is identical,
Being the crowned one in each of us,
The sword each free adorer raises,
The divinity each impassioned chariot
Rushes, perpetually, toward.

Among the Barbarians

Within the sea of sorrow my sphere of light shines serene.
Madness cannot penetrate locked glass,
Nor can the cruel, the ignorant,
Spill—nor shatter—
My cup of joy.

Still, a lonely cry
Greets me
In my solitary temple
—Why is love despised
And beauty scorned?

Note:

Compare line 2 with *The Book of the Law* III:10.

This Thing and I

I do not need
This hideous Thing
That cries so ferociously
For justice.

There is no justice
(This Thing and I agree on that).

"But there should be, there *will* be,"
Cries this Thing that paces in my cell
And counts out wrongs (not imaginary)
That burn its fingers with their ugliness.

"There is no justice," I return.
(I feel its flame, its bitterness.)
"But there is joy,
  Grey-eyed, contented joy,
  Protecting those
  Whose Truth is bliss."

A Lover of the Wing'd Self, Among Those Who Merely See

I worship among the shadows,
I shine within the house of death,
For beauty, intense, eternal, is He with whom I choose to mate
—Not consciously, this choice. I know too well the price
On bitter earth. But a higher,
More fulfilling self says Yes
To that shining, soul-contenting gold
Whenever—Oh!—his face draws near.

As to the others, the trouble is they do not see
This one I mate with
(Nor, I suspect, my utterly adoring eye)
Nor do they allow (how could they?)
For my pregnancy and time of birth;
The worst, however, is when my child is born
And they see it as a nothing,
A mere waste, a foolishness.

The images the others see me as
—it frightens me—
The dim, at times,
Have trampling and self-righteous feet.

But (all that aside)
Am I not content with Him I choose,
With the bliss of being wife,
With the joy of being mother?

Of course.

Then worship Him you worship,
Mate, give birth,
And watch with perfect eye
The shining of your children.

Book III:

Fulfillment

To be a sunlit Zero in all the realms!
To quietly shine with beauty's contented eye!

Praise to the Impersonal God

Circle of Night

Circle of night
—Unbroken bliss—
Within which every heart is one,
I respect your oneness,
I respect your innocent fire.

Meditation of a Warrior-Priest

Ugly ones with hearts of gold
Crowd about my tent.
I welcome gladly hearts of gold;
I cannot welcome ugliness.

His Reply to One of Wealth Whose Way of Dust Rewarded with a Silken Bed

—A tent?
Because the palace and society
Pale against the joy of love and death.

To a Moralist

Death is inevitable;
What better than to die
To what you love?

Sanity

I love intimately;
I let go intimately.
The sanity of joyous passion
Rules my war, my worship,
And my ecstasy.

Praise to the Impersonal God

Beauty is so simple
As the standard of motion;
Love is so easy
As the unmoved ground.
Pan remains,
The God of the loving;
His core is golden
Though His face is brown.

Joy Is the Holy Circle

Ten Years Ago

Ten years ago I fell in love
(The circle opened,
 And I was one within).

But he was one too beautiful for my hope,
And I fell out, and stumbled,
And cracked my shin.

But whenever we have seen the one we shine to,
However distant or not our own,
Invisible as the eyes that touch him,
He becomes our unseen home.

Eros

Eros,
I trust your arrow;
With surprise, I note who brings
The fire.

The Garden

May I remember the Garden
—It is within ourselves.
From where else can come
The apple of contentment,
The tree of delight?

The world is mad,
Mechanical and greedy for dust;
Love's law and love's temple
Are, as yet, silent and unseen.

Caduceus

Out of love
Rise the serpents of desire,
Whose wrestling bodies
Are the fire of innocence.

Private Taste

Private taste, apparently,
Is the glory of freedom
—How amazing, then,
The universality of joy!

To the Crowned Ones of Despair

Not sorrow, but joy, is the great
Mystery.

Joy Is the Holy Circle

Joy is the holy circle, contentment is the holy circle
(The temple and the palace of the genuine fire);
Neither flesh nor contract
(The visible, the forced)
Has meaning
Where the royal chariot—Great Mother!—
Has passed it by.

The Juggler

The Juggler

The Juggler, freely shining,
One with the blue of heaven,
Remains balanced above the pit of nothingness,
Where mechanisms rattle onward,
Madness reigns,
And the body of light lies scattered.

The Filth of Ambition

The filth of ambition
Is, precisely, that—but its angel
Is the star-bright hand that reaches only
For the apples of Hesperides.

Perfect Machinery

Perfect machinery does not impress me.
What is it but the dead,
Well fitting, well oiled,
Whirling swiftly—*where?*—
Under the pressure of a dead force?

Only the gods, only the shining ones,
Can wake such blind immensities
—Such hapless particles—
To that freedom, that central radiance: each shining self.

Reality

Just as government occurs only where the soul is noble,
Reality occurs only where one is oneself.

Chaste Flesh

Wisdom

Forgive utterly;
Love fully;
Create freely;
Shine unhesitantly.

Chaste Flesh

Chaste flesh,
Eros awaits you—eternity unwinds
Her ceaseless thread—
In a time when joy to joy
Is freely wed.

I Forgive

I forgive,
And I burn toward
The sun of my desire.

Advice from the Wing'd Globe

Fulfillment

Fulfillment,
Not the climbing of mountains,
Is achievement.

Advice from the Wing'd Globe

Cast the filth from the sacred sphere!
Love, still, is the shining Lawyer
Where burning joy lifts the horns of the Ram;
Beauty of self claims the Goat
When we stand on the simple waters of the Crab.

Forthcoming:

The Sword of Time

Book IV:
Thing and Righteousness

Book V:
Jehovah Unbound

by
Hank Fisher